CuteCookies

50 simply scrumptious recipes

CuteCookies

50 simply scrumptious recipes

VINCENT SQUARE BOOKS

First published in Great Britain in 2011 by
Vincent Square Books
an imprint of Kyle Books
www.kylebooks.com

ISBN 978 0 85783 047 0

A Cataloguing in Publication record for this title is available from the British Library.

10 9 8 7 6 5 4 3 2 1

Design **Geoff Hayes**
Series Design **Nicky Collings**
Project Editors **Vicky Orchard and Estella Hung**
Production **Nic Jones and David Hearn**

Colour reproduction by Scanhouse in Malaysia
Printed and bound in China by C&C Offset Printing Co., Ltd

Contents

Introduction

From the classic Jammy Dodgers (page 12) to the decadent Chocolate-drenched Cocoa-nib Cookies (page 84) and the healthier Orange Tuiles (page 66) this is a collection of cookies for all tastes and occasions. Savoury and sweet, these biscuits look as good as they taste and the recipes provide a wide and inspiring range of baked treats, including vegan and gluten-free options such as Peach Biscuits (page 58) and Chocolate, Peanut Butter & Fudge Cookies (page 37). Gluten-free recipes throughout are marked with a GF symbol and vegan ones with a V so they are easy to identify.

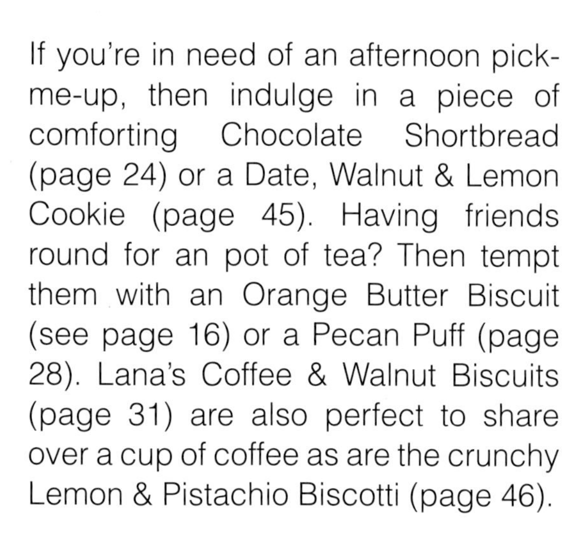

If you're in need of an afternoon pick-me-up, then indulge in a piece of comforting Chocolate Shortbread (page 24) or a Date, Walnut & Lemon Cookie (page 45). Having friends round for an pot of tea? Then tempt them with an Orange Butter Biscuit (see page 16) or a Pecan Puff (page 28). Lana's Coffee & Walnut Biscuits (page 31) are also perfect to share over a cup of coffee as are the crunchy Lemon & Pistachio Biscotti (page 46).

For when you're seeking a healthier option there's also a wide variety of recipes to choose from (Chapter 2). Soft Pine Nut Cookies (page 57) are a lighter option and also suitable for coealics as are the Gluten-Free Almond Jam Cookies (page 62), which

also have the added bonus of being suitable for vegans too, so nobody has to miss out.

If it's a savoury rather than sweet craving that you're trying to satisfy then there are also plenty of options: Parmesan Shortbread (page 73) are the perfect accompaniment to an aperitif or replacement for canapes with cocktails, while the classic Oatmeal Crackers (page 77) are the ideal way to round off a meal alongside a selection of cheese and chutneys.

Cookies are also a great alternative to a more traditional pudding after a main course or when you want a dessert suitable for more informal entertaining. Brown Caramel Biscuits (page 83) provide a more unusual option while Double Dark Chocolate, Pecan & Ginger Cookies (page 91) deliver a crunch and sweetness that will satisfy even the most demanding dinner guest. And if you can't decide between a sweet dessert or cheese then Chocolate Water Biscuits for Cheese (page 94) are a perfect compromise.

Festive celebrations require something a bit special so there's Star of Bethlehem Biscuits (page 113) to get into the Christmas spirit and Stained Glass Snowflake Cookies (page 114) that can be hung on the tree or from a window so their beautiful decoration catches the light. Cinnamon Spice & All Things Nice Cookies (page 109) are full of festive flavours and for something a bit different you can make Fortune Cookies (page 99) to see in the New Year with style.

Hints & tips for perfect cookies every time

Make sure your ingredients, particularly dairy (butter, milk, yogurt etc.) are at room temperature before you begin preparing your cookies.

It is important to measure all the ingredients accurately. Baking is a chemical reaction so quantities need to be correct. Check that your scales are accurate from time to time (test them with a can of chopped tomatoes or something similar that has a given weight). Digital scales are more accurate than spring scales and some can also measure in mililitres as well as grams so are useful for measuring liquid ingredients too.

Before you start to bake it's a good idea to clear and clean an area of worktop large enough for you to roll out the cookie dough on.

Being prepared will save you time and making the baking process much smoother. Have a good look at the ingredients and any special equipment that you need to make your cookies, and gather it all together before you begin.

Quality does matter – use the best quality ingredients that you can as this will make a difference to the end flavour of your cookies. If a recipe calls for baking powder, bicarbonate of soda or cream of tartar check that they aren't past their expiry date. – these can all sit unused at the back of the cupboard for quite a while if it's been some time since the last time you baked.

When making cookie dough, try not to handle it any more than you need to as this makes it tough and will affect the texture of your cookies.

A lot of cookie doughs can be made and frozen ahead of time. You can shape the dough into a log, wrap, chill or freeze until it's time to bake or you can form the cookie dough into balls, freeze and then bake straight from frozen, adding a few minutes to the stated baking time. This technique also lets you make all the dough one day, then take another day for baking and decorating if the recipe requires.

Don't overload the oven. Bake one baking tray of cookies at a time on the middle shelf of the oven. If you do need to bake more than one tray at a time then rotate the trays between shelves halfway through baking to encourage even browning.

Be careful with overbaking. Check whether the cookies are done at the minimum stated baking time or a few minutes before.

If you're short on cooling racks place a sheet of baking parchment on the counter and sprinkle it with sugar. Cookies will cool without getting soggy.

Make sure you cool cookies completely before storing them in airtight containers.

Afternoon Tea

Jammy Dodgers

In order to obtain the most perfectly shaped hole for the jam to fit in this biscuit, you should make the shape just before baking and fill it only halfway through cooking. Feel free to use strawberry, apricot or raspberry jam.

115g plain flour
30g semolina
a pinch of salt
¼ teaspoon ground cinnamon
a scant ¼ teaspoon ground cloves
115g unsalted butter, softened
70g soft light brown sugar
1 egg yolk
1 teaspoon vanilla extract
3–4 teaspoons strawberry jam

Preheat the oven to 180°C/350°F/gas mark 4.

Sift the flour, semolina, salt and spices into a mixing bowl. In another bowl, beat together the butter and sugar until creamy and soft. Add the egg yolk and vanilla, and stir well.

Add the dry ingredients to the butter mixture and combine to a soft dough. With floured hands, divide the mixture into 12–15 small balls (about the size of walnuts).

Place the balls on a lightly greased baking tray and flatten the tops slightly. Using the tip of your thumb or the handle of a wooden spoon, make a little depression on the top of each biscuit. Put in the oven for 10 minutes, then remove and fill each little hole with a tiny amount of jam. Return to the oven for a further 10–12 minutes, or until golden brown.

Transfer at once to a wire rack to cool completely before serving. Store in an airtight container.

Vanilla Cookie Sandwiches

Galliano liqueur is strongly flavoured with vanilla, so it complements the vanilla in the actual cookie. If you don't have any, substitute it with vanilla extract.

Makes 8

3 eggs
85g caster sugar
115ml vegetable oil
2 teaspoons baking powder
1½ teaspoons vanilla extract
285g plain flour

For the filling:
285ml crème fraîche
1 tablespoon Galliano liqueur

Preheat the oven to 150°C/300°F/gas mark 2.

Using a balloon whisk, beat together the eggs, sugar, oil, baking powder and vanilla. Once smooth, sift in the flour, and fold gently together with a wooden spoon to combine.

Using two teaspoons, drop 16 blobs of the mixture onto a lightly greased baking tray. Bake in the oven for about 20 minutes or until cooked through and a pale golden brown. Transfer at once to a wire rack and allow to cool.

Once cooled, prepare the filling. Add the Galliano to the crème fraîche and stir until smooth. Sandwich two cookies together with the creamy filling. They are best assembled just before eating, although they will hold well (without becoming too soggy) for about an hour.

Orange Butter Biscuits

So simple to make and bake, and so simple to eat a whole batch in an afternoon. Delicious accompanied with a cup of tea.

Makes 40

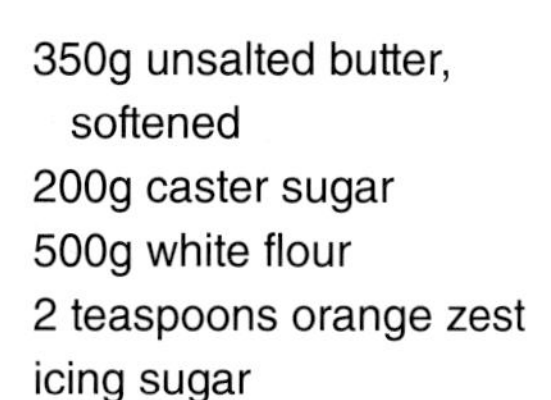

350g unsalted butter, softened
200g caster sugar
500g white flour
2 teaspoons orange zest
icing sugar

Preheat the oven to 160°C/325°F/gas mark 3.

Whizz the butter with the caster sugar, flour and orange zest in a food processor for a few seconds to make a soft dough.

Roll into walnut-sized balls and flatten slightly. Arrange on a baking tray about 2.5cm apart (they will spread out).

Bake for about 25 minutes. They should still be pale – not at all coloured. They will seem very soft and uncooked, but they will firm up as they cool. Remove from the baking tray only when they have firmed up.

Dredge in icing sugar.

Nut & Butter Biscuits

You can customise these tasty little treats with any type of nut you fancy – pecans, hazelnuts or blanched almonds work particularly well.

Makes 

350g unsalted butter, softened
200g caster sugar
500g white flour
40 of your choice of nuts (pecans, hazelnuts or blanched almonds)
icing sugar

Preheat the oven to 160°C/325°F/gas mark 3.

Whizz the butter with the caster sugar and flour in a food processor for a few seconds to make a soft dough.

Roll into walnut-sized balls and flatten slightly.

Arrange on a baking tray about 2.5cm apart (they will spread out). Press a pecan, hazelnut or blanched almond on top of each ball before baking.

Bake for about 25 minutes. They should still be pale – not at all coloured. They will seem very soft and uncooked, but they will firm up when they cool. Remove from the baking tray only when they have firmed up.

Dredge in icing sugar.

Chocolate Meringue 'S' Biscuits

These are a mainstay of almost every pastry shop in Switzerland. An 'S' shape is traditional for these, but of course you may pipe them into any shape you wish.

Makes 40–50

4 medium egg whites
pinch of salt
280g sugar
140g dark chocolate (70–75% cocoa solids), melted and slightly cooled

Half-fill a saucepan on which your mixer bowl will fit without having more than 5cm water inside the pan. Bring the water to the boil over a low heat.

Place the egg whites in the bowl, and with a hand-held electric whisk, whisk to break them up. Whisk in the salt and sugar.

Set the bowl over the pan of water so only a small part of the base is submerged and whisk gently to keep the mixture moving so that it doesn't set on the bottom; whisking too vigorously can tighten the mixture and prevent the sugar form melting. Continue whisking until the egg whites are hot (54°C) and the sugar has dissolved. Lift the whisk and let a little of the mixture run over a fingertip to test the temperature and smoothness. While heating the mixture, occasionally scrape the side of the bowl with a rubber spatula to keep the sugar from accumulating there.

Whisk the mixture on medium-high speed until the meringue has increased in volume and looks like a marshmallow, which will take about 3 minutes.

Stop whisking when the side of the bowl feels just slightly warm.

Use a large rubber spatula to fold the melted chocolate into the meringue. Be careful not to fold so much that the meringue liquefies from contact with the fat in the chocolate. If a few streaks of white remain, ignore them.

Half-fill a pastry bag fitted with a 1.25cm star tip (Ateco size 4) and pipe the meringue onto two baking trays or Swiss roll tins, lined with baking parchment, in 'S' shapes: hold the bag almost perpendicular to the tin and inclined slightly towards you with the end of the tube close to the tin. Start to squeeze out an 'S' shape; when you come to the end, pull away parallel to the tin, not straight upward, to avoid leaving a point.

After piping the biscuits, let them dry at room temperature for a couple of hours so they retain their shape better and they form the characteristic 'foot' at the bottom. About 20 minutes before you're ready to bake the biscuits, arrange shelves in the upper and lower thirds of the oven and preheat to 180°C/350°F/gas mark 4.

Bake the biscuits until they are matt-looking but still a little moist within (press one with a fingertip), 8–10 minutes. Cool on the tins on racks.

Breton Butter Biscuits

This crumbly biscuit from Brittany is traditionally a plain biscuit which has so much butter in it any other flavour seems superfluous. This ultra-indulgent recipe rivals the traditional English chocolate digestive with a coating of chocolate.

Makes  50

375g plain flour
large pinch of salt
150g caster sugar
200g unsalted butter, chilled and diced
1 large egg, lightly beaten
½ teaspoon vanilla extract
200g milk chocolate or 50g each of milk, dark, good-quality dark orange chocolate, and white chocolate, broken into pieces for dipping

Preheat the oven to 160°C/325°F/gas mark 3. Grease a large baking tray.

Sift together the flour and the salt. Add the sugar and butter and process in a food processor or rub between your fingertips until the mixture resembles breadcrumbs. Add the egg and the vanilla extract and process again or mix together with your hands until the mixture comes together as a firm dough. Wrap in clingfilm and chill for at least 15 minutes.

Roll out on a lightly floured board to a thickness of about 3mm. Cut out the biscuits using a fluted cutter. Place on the baking tray and bake the biscuits for 15–20 minutes until light golden brown. Cool on a wire rack.

Once the biscuits have cooled, melt the chocolate in a heatproof bowl suspended over a saucepan of barely simmering water. If using one flavour of chocolate, select a bowl that will allow you to fit your hand into it so that you can dip the biscuits. Be very careful when melting the white chocolate and ensure that the bowl does not touch the water as the chocolate will become thick and lumpy easily. If you are using different flavours of chocolate, once melted, pour the chocolate onto a small plate and dip the surface of each biscuit in the chocolate before returning them to the wire rack to set.

The biscuits can simply have one surface dipped in the chocolate or you could decorate by drizzling white chocolate over a biscuit previously dipped in dark or white chocolate. You can also dip only half the biscuit with chocolate.

Chocolate Shortbread

How can you better a basic shortbread recipe? Add chocolate! If you mix carefully, the chocolate chunks should remain more or less whole and only melt a little into the shortbread. The result is a crumbly, buttery biscuit bulging with chocolate. Serve with a cup of tea or coffee, or even for dessert with some creamy vanilla or nutty ice cream.

Makes 

285g unsalted butter, softened
170g caster sugar
170g milk chocolate (minimum 30% cocoa solids), cut into chunks
225g plain flour, sifted
115g semolina

Preheat the oven to 150°C/300°F/gas mark 2.

Lightly grease a 23 x 33cm Swiss roll tin. Beat the softened butter and sugar in a bowl using an electric whisk (on the lowest speed), until light and fluffy. This takes only a couple of minutes.

Add the chocolate chunks, then the flour and semolina. Using a wooden spoon, combine everything together. Do no overbeat or stir vigorously at this stage, or you will end up with tough shortbread. Your mixture should be slightly crumbly but thoroughly combined.

Turn into the prepared tin and, using the palms of your hands, press the mixture down well into the tin. You may need to lightly flour your hands, depending on how warm they are. Most biscuits and shortbread cook more evenly if pricked with a fork all over.

Bake in the oven for about 40 minutes, or until golden brown around the edges. Cut into squares or fingers while still hot and leave to cool in the tin for 30–40 minutes. Using a large fish slice, transfer to a wire rack to cool completely before eating.

Vanilla Almond Fluted Biscuits

These biscuits can be made into the traditional wreath-shape. If you're keen to try the traditional route, you'll need an old-fashioned meat mincer with a star-shaped hole to make the long, fluted sausages, which are then shaped into wreaths. Alternatively, simply roll lengths of the dough and twist to a coil and cut.

- 250g blanched almonds
- 1–2 vanilla pods, finely chopped
- 250g plain flour
- 1 teaspoon baking powder
- 250g sugar
- 125g salted butter
- 2 eggs

Run the almonds and vanilla pods through a food processor until they resemble fine breadcrumbs. Put all the ingredients into a bowl big enough to hold everything and knead to a smooth dough. Let it rest in a cool place until the next day.

Preheat the oven to 180°C/350°F/gas mark 4. Now run the dough through the meat-mincer, without the knife attached, but with the disc with a star-shaped hole in it. If this is unavailable, any hole will do. You will need two people to do this, one to receive the long strands of biscuit dough and shape them on parchment paper, and one to crank the handle and feed the mincer.

Bake in the preheated oven until pale golden.

Pecan Puffs

Pecan lovers will delight in these delicious morsels that are packed with pecan flavour but without the chunks.

110g butter
2 tablespoons caster sugar
150g pecans, finely ground
150g plain white flour, sifted
½ teaspoon vanilla extract
icing sugar

Preheat the oven to 150°C/300°F/gas mark 2.

Cream the butter, add the sugar and beat until soft and light. Mix the nuts in with the butter and sugar, and add the flour and vanilla extract.

Pinch off teaspoonfuls of the mixture and roll into balls. Place well apart on greased baking trays.

Bake for 30 minutes or until pale and golden.

Remove from the oven. Handle very carefully as they will be fragile, brittle and very hot. Cool on a wire rack.

Dredge with icing sugar and store in an airtight container.

Lana's Coffee & Walnut Biscuits

Inspired by the classic coffee and walnut cake these biscuits use the same combination of flavours but provide a crunchier alternative.

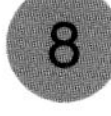

Makes 8

175g flour
75g butter
50g caster sugar
1 organic egg, whisked
8 fresh walnut halves, to decorate

For the coffee filling:
25g butter
50g icing sugar, sieved
1 teaspoon Irel or Camp coffee essence

For the coffee icing:
110g icing sugar, sieved
scant ½ tablespoon Irel or Camp coffee essence
about 1 tablespoon boiling water

Preheat the oven to 180°C/350°F/gas mark 4.

Sift the flour into a bowl. Rub in the butter, add the sugar and mix well. Mix the dry ingredients to a stiff dough with the whisked egg.

Turn onto a floured board and roll out to a 2.5mm thickness. Cut into rounds using a 8.5cm cutter. Bake until golden brown, about 8 minutes. Transfer to a wire rack and leave to cool.

Meanwhile, make the coffee filling and icing. Cream the butter, then add the icing sugar and coffee essence. Continue to whisk until light and fluffy.

To make the icing, put the sieved icing sugar into a bowl. Add coffee essence and enough boiling water to make it the consistency of a very thick cream. Whisk until smooth and glossy.

Sandwich the biscuits together with the coffee filling and spread a little coffee icing on top. Then decorate each biscuit with a walnut half.

Aztec Cookies

These cookies have it all – sweet fruit, chewy nuts and bitter chocolate. Keep your chunks large to maximise the flavour.

Makes 22–24

115g dried apricots (no-soak variety), roughly chopped
115g dark chocolate, roughly chopped
170g walnuts, roughly chopped
285g dessicated coconut
1 x 400g can of sweetened condensed milk

Preheat the oven to 160°C/325°F/gas mark 3.

Roughly chop the apricots, chocolate and nuts. Place everything together in a large mixing bowl and, using a wooden spoon, beat together until thoroughly mixed.

Using 2 tablespoons, drop about 20 blobs of the mixture onto a greased baking tray and gently flatten down the tops.

Bake in the oven for about 20 minutes, or until golden brown. Transfer at once to a wire rack to cool.

Anzac Biscuits

These are traditionally eaten on Anzac Day (25 April) in Australia and New Zealand. They were introduced during the First World War as a tribute to the Australian and New Zealand forces, who fought in the invasion of the Gallipoli peninsula in 1915. The biscuits are crunchy, buttery and crisp: delicious with a cup of frothy hot chocolate.

170g unsalted butter
1 tablespoon golden syrup
1 teaspoon bicarbonate of soda
1 tablespoon boiling water
115g rolled oats (jumbo oatflakes)
115g plain flour, sifted
55g dessicated coconut
115g caster sugar

Preheat the oven to 160°C/325°F/gas mark 3. Lightly grease a baking tray.

Melt the butter and syrup in a large saucepan over a low heat. Dissolve the bicarbonate of soda in the water, then stir into the melted mixture.

Mix together the remaining ingredients in a separate bowl and turn into the saucepan. Stir well to combine.

Using dessertspoons, place small spoonfuls of the mixture onto the baking tray. Bake in the oven for 15–20 minutes, or until a light golden brown.

Cool for 2 minutes on the tray, then transfer to a wire rack to cool completely.

Chocolate, Peanut Butter & Fudge Cookies

This recipe is so simple it's unbelievable – just mix together well and bake! It also has the bonus of using no flour at all. If you slightly undercook the cookies you will end up with a softer, chewier texture, but if you prefer your cookies slightly crunchier, bake a little longer.

Makes  12–14  GF Gluten-free

1 medium egg, at room temperature
80g caster sugar
125g crunchy peanut butter, at room temperature
pinch or two of chilli powder
40g hard fudge, finely chopped
40g dark chocolate, finely chopped

Preheat the oven to 180°C/350°F/gas mark 4. Line two baking trays with baking parchment (you will need to cook these in batches).

Place the egg and sugar in a bowl and break up with a whisk. Add the peanut butter and chilli powder and mix well. Add the chopped fudge and chocolate and mix in.

Spoon heaped dessertspoons of the mixture onto the lined baking trays and spread out slightly, as the mixture will not spread much during the baking time, then bake for 12–14 minutes.

When cooked, remove the cookies from the paper with a palette knife and cool on a wire rack.

Store the cooled biscuits in an airtight container for up to 1 week.

The cooked, cooled cookies freeze well. Wrap well and store in an airtight container. Defrost for 30 minutes, then heat through at 180°C/350°F/gas mark 4 for 2–3 minutes to soften again.

Chocolate Digestive Biscuits

Delicious on their own but also great when making pie crusts, these digestive biscuits have all-natural ingredients and don't have the high-fructose corn syrup like shop-bought brands.

Makes  30  GF Gluten-free

- 65g unbleached flour
- 195g wholewheat flour
- ½ cup evaporated cane juice, divided
- 50g cocoa powder
- ½ teaspoon salt
- 1 teaspoon baking powder
- 55g butter substitute
- 2 tablespoons light agave nectar
- 1 tablespoon molasses or black treacle
- 60ml water

Preheat the oven to 180°C/350°F/gas mark 4. Line two baking trays with aluminum foil or baking parchment.

Using a stand mixer, combine the flours, half of the cane juice, the cocoa powder, salt, and baking powder. With the motor running on a medium speed, add the butter substitute 1 tablespoon at a time, waiting 10 seconds after each addition. Continue mixing for about 1 minute until the mixture resembles coarse sand.

In a small bowl, combine the agave nectar, molasses, and water. Add to the flour mixture and mix for about 1 minute until it forms a ball of dough. Wrap in clingfilm and chill for 1 hour in the refrigerator.

Lightly flour your work surface, rolling pin, and the ball of chilled dough. Roll the dough out as thinly as possible. Using a knife, cut the dough into squares, or use any shaped biscuit cutter. Place the biscuits on the prepared baking trays, about 2.5cm apart. Prick with a fork, lightly brush with water and sprinkle with the remaining cane juice.

Bake for 13–15 minutes until the biscuits are crisp. Store in an airtight container for up to 2 weeks.

Mother-in-Law's Tongues

The stereotypical 'sharpness' of a mother-in-law's tongue is provided by some bitter marmalade; sweeter jams, such as raspberry or blackcurrant, can be used for 'sweeter' mother-in-laws!

Makes 

250g plain flour
100g caster sugar
100g butter
2 organic egg yolks
50–75g bitter marmalade or lemon or lime marmalade

Preheat the oven to 180°C/350°F/gas mark 4.

Put the flour, sugar and diced butter in a food processor. Pulse a few times, and then add the egg yolks and a drop of water – just enough to bring the dough together.

Turn out, flatten into a round and wrap in greaseproof paper. Rest in the fridge for about 30 minutes.

Flour the worktop and roll out the dough to a thickness of 5mm. Stamp ovals with a 9 x 7cm oval cutter. Transfer to a baking tray. Spoon a small blob of bitter marmalade into the centre of each oval. Pinch the long ends together so they meet in the centre to cover the marmalade.

Bake for 10–15 minutes in the oven. When golden, transfer to a wire rack. Dust with icing sugar when cool.

Lemon Cookies

Don't keep these buttery biscuits with a zing of citrus for yourself – packaged simply, they make excellent gifts for all ages and occasions.

200g unsalted butter
120g icing sugar
1 egg yolk
zest of 2 lemons
2 teaspoons lemon juice
250g plain flour
caster sugar, for sprinkling

Cream the butter and sugar in an electric mixer until soft and creamy. Add the egg yolk, beat until smooth, then add the lemon zest, juice and flour. Continue to mix until all the dough ingredients are well combined.

Cover the work surface with a sheet of cling film and place the dough on top; cover with a second sheet of cling film. Roll the dough to a thickness of 7mm.

Place in the fridge for 1 hour.

Preheat the oven 180°C/350°F/gas mark 4. Line a baking tray with baking parchment. Lightly flour a cool work surface. Transfer the dough from the fridge to the floured surface and use a heart-shaped cutter to cut out about 20 hearts, placing them on the baking tray.

Bake for about 10 minutes or until the heart shapes turn a golden colour. Transfer the hearts onto a cooling rack and sprinkle with caster sugar. When cold, pack carefully in airtight containers.

Date, Walnut & Lemon Cookies

These little cookies are golden on the outside, yet slightly soft in the centre – perfect for a reasonably healthy snack to serve with tea or coffee. They'd also work well with other firm-textured dried fruit, such as figs, or with any other nuts.

150g dates
75g walnuts
75g lightly salted butter, cut into cubes, plus extra for greasing
1 tablespoon clear honey or golden syrup
finely grated zest of 1 lemon
100g fine oatmeal
25g self-raising flour
3 tablespoons Splenda granulated sweetener
1 teaspoon vanilla extract
1 egg, beaten
extra oatmeal, for dusting

Preheat the oven to 220°C/425°F/gas mark 7. Grease a large baking tray.

Whizz the dates in a food processor until chopped into small pieces. Add the walnuts and blend again until chopped.

Melt the butter in a medium saucepan with the honey or syrup and lemon zest. Tip the dates and walnuts, oatmeal, flour, sweetener and vanilla and stir until mixed. Add the egg and beat to a thick paste.

Take spoonfuls of the mixture and shape into balls. Flatten onto the baking tray, spacing them slightly apart. Sprinkle with extra oatmeal and pop into the oven.

Bake for 10 minutes or until golden brown around the edges. Transfer to a wire rack to cool.

Lemon & Pistachio Biscotti

Don't keep these crisp Italian biscuits for after dinner treats with coffee – they can be enjoyed any time and even as a dessert with ice cream.

Makes 16

250g plain flour
1 teaspoon baking powder
175g caster sugar
pinch of salt
2 eggs
grated zest of 3 lemons
1 tablespoon lemon juice
100g blanched almonds, toasted and chopped
50g pistachios, chopped

Preheat the oven to 180°C/350°F/gas mark 4. Lightly flour a baking tray.

Place all the ingredients in a mixing bowl and mix to form a firm dough. Roll into a ball, cut in half and roll each portion into a sausage shape before placing on a lightly floured baking tray.

Place in the preheated oven for 10 minutes. Remove from the oven, cool for 5 minutes, then use a serrated knife to cut into diagonal slices, 1cm thick.

Arrange the slices on the baking tray and return to the oven for a further 15 minutes to turn slightly golden. Transfer to a wire rack to allow to cool and crisp up. These biscotti keep well in an airtight container for up to a week.

Orange & Almond Biscotti

These will keep for up to two weeks in an airtight container, so you can make them ahead of time. They are also delicious halved and then dipped in melted chocolate.

Makes 

- 250g plain flour
- ½ teaspoon baking powder
- ½ teaspoon bicarbonate of soda
- 115g unsalted butter, softened
- 150g caster sugar
- 2 large eggs
- 2 tablespoons grated orange zest
- 1 tablespoon orange juice
- 150g whole almonds

Preheat the oven to 180°C/350°F/gas mark 4. Lightly flour a baking tray.

Sift all the dry ingredients, except for the sugar and almonds, into a large bowl and mix well.

In a separate bowl, using an electric mixer on medium speed, cream together the butter and sugar until light and fluffy. Beat in the eggs, one at a time, then tip in the orange zest and juice. Stir into the flour mixture and almonds until the dough comes together.

With floured hands, divide the dough in half. Shape each half into a log and place the logs on a baking tray with 7.5cm between them. Pat into 7.5cm wide loaves.

Bake in the oven for 30 minutes or until the dough is firm to the touch. Transfer the loaves to a cutting board. Leave the oven on. Using a serrated knife, cut each loaf crosswise on the diagonal into 1cm slices. Arrange the slices in one layer on a baking tray. Return to the oven and bake for 10 minutes. Turn the biscotti over and bake for a further 10 minutes.

Transfer the biscotti to wire racks to cool. Store in layers in an airtight container.

Lavender Biscuits

The delicate lavender notes of these simple to make biscuits provide a lovely fragrant smell as well as flavour.

Makes 20

- 100g butter
- 50g caster sugar
- 175g self-raising flour
- 2 tablespoons fresh lavender leaves, chopped
- 1 teaspoon lavender flowers, removed from spike

Preheat the oven to 230°C/450°F/gas mark 8. Grease a baking tray.

Cream the butter and sugar together until light. Add the flour and lavender leaves to the butter mixture. Knead well until it forms a dough.

Gently roll out on a lightly floured board. Scatter the flowers over the rolled dough and lightly press in with the rolling pin.

Cut into small rounds with a cutter. Place the biscuits on a greased baking tray. Bake for 10–12 minutes until golden and firm. Remove at once and cool on a wire rack.

Healthier Choices

Soft Zesty Lemon Fondant Cookies

Making up the topping for these zesty cookies using fondant icing sugar with lemon juice gives the icing a really acidic kick. Fondant icing sugar is icing sugar with glucose added, so it sets at room temperature with a lovely shine, similar to the long iced buns you can buy at bakeries.

Makes  12  GF Gluten-free

For the gluten-free flour mix (makes 200g):
140g fine white rice flour
40g potato flour
20g tapioca flour

80g cooking margarine
¼ teaspoon baking powder
pinch of salt
75g caster sugar
1 medium egg, at room temperature
1 teaspoon glycerine
zest of 1 large lemon

For the icing:
juice of 1 large lemon
50g fondant icing sugar
extra lemon zest, to decorate

Mix all the flours together very thoroughly or put into a food processor and pulse until mixed.

Then place the flour mixture, margarine, baking powder, salt and sugar into a food processor and blitz until you have achieved the consistency of fine breadcrumbs. Add the egg, glycerine and lemon zest and mix. Lightly bring together on a floured surface, and then form into a 15–20cm long sausage. Wrap in clingfilm and chill well.

Preheat the oven to 200°C/400°F/gas mark 6. Line two baking trays with baking parchment (you will need to cook these in batches).

When you are ready to bake the cookies, cut off 5–8mm slices of the dough and place them on the lined trays. Bake for 15–20 minutes or until cooked and lightly browned. Then transfer to a wire rack to cool.

Meanwhile, put the lemon juice in a small bowl, then add the fondant icing sugar and beat until smooth. You may need to adjust the consistency with a little water (softer) or extra fondant icing sugar (firmer). Coat the cookies thickly with the icing, decorate with lemon zest and leave to set.

Store the cooled biscuits in an airtight container for up to 1 week. The dough and the cooked un-iced cookies also freeze well.

For the dough: Wrap it in clingfilm and freeze. Defrost for 1 hour or until soft enough to cut and cook as above.

For the cookies: Wrap well and store in an airtight container. Defrost for 30 minutes, then heat through at 180°C/350°F/gas mark 4 for 2–3 minutes to soften again. Ice once cooled.

Soft Pine Nut Cookies

This is a delicious gluten-free version of the meringue biscuit found in northern Italy. It's light and packed full of flavour.

Makes 20  Gluten-free

200g flaked almonds
100g pine nuts
100g rice flour
225g caster sugar
zest of 1 lemon
2 medium egg whites, at room temperature
pinch of cream of tartar
½ teaspoon vanilla extract
½ teaspoon almond extract
cinnamon and sieved icing sugar, for dusting

Preheat the oven to 180°C/350°F/gas mark 4. Line a baking tray with baking parchment.

Place the almonds and pine nuts on the lined tray, and brown them well in the oven for 8–10 minutes; the almonds will brown slightly quicker. Once browned, remove from the oven and cool. Reduce the oven temperature to 160°C/325°F/gas mark 3.

Once cooled, place the almonds and rice flour in a food processor and blitz until you have a fine mix. Place into a medium mixing bowl, add the pine nuts, 115g of the sugar and the lemon zest, and mix well.

Whisk the egg whites with the cream of tartar until light and foamy, then add the remaining caster sugar and whisk until creamy and glossy, but do not overbeat. Mix the nut mixture into the egg whites, along with the vanilla and almond extracts.

Using two wetted teaspoons, mould the mixture into small oval mounds and place on the lined tray (you will need to cook these in batches). Pat each mound down slightly before baking.

Bake for 15–20 minutes until they turn light golden, keeping an eye on them as they brown quickly. Remove and transfer to a wire rack to cool.

Sprinkle with cinnamon and icing sugar.

Store the cooled biscuits in an airtight container for up to 1 week. Freeze the cooled cookies before dusting with the sugar and cinnamon – wrap well and store in an airtight container. Defrost for 30 minutes, then heat through at 180°C/350°F/gas mark 4 for 2–3 minutes to soften again and then dust with the sugar and cinnamon.

Peach Biscuits

So delicious on a hot summer day, these biscuits are great served for brunch or dessert.

Makes  10  V Vegan

For the biscuits:
260g unbleached plain flour
2 teaspoons baking powder
½ teaspoon salt
55g butter substitute
180ml soya milk

For the fruit topping:
4 large peaches
3 tablespoons apricot conserve or jam
1 tablespoon water

For the coating:
170g evaporated cane juice
2 teaspoons ground cinnamon
335g butter substitute

Preheat the oven to 190°C/375°F/gas mark 5.

First make the biscuits. Using a stand mixer, combine the flour, baking powder, and salt on a medium speed. With the motor still running, add the butter substitute 1 tablespoon at a time, waiting 5 seconds after each addition. Add the soya milk and beat the mixture on a medium speed until a soft dough has formed. Turn the dough out onto a lightly floured work surface, and roll out until 1cm thick. Cut out biscuits with a 10cm round cutter. Re-roll the dough trimmings and cut out more biscuits. Set aside.

Wash and dry the peaches, the halve, discard the stones and cut into 5mm thick slices. Set aside.

To make the coating, mix together the cane juice and cinnamon in a medium bowl. Melt the butter substitute in a microwave-safe bowl in the microwave for 1 minute. Dip the biscuits into the melted butter, then in the cinnamon sugar, and place on a 25 × 38cm baking tray.

Create a well in each biscuit. Arrange the sliced peaches, slightly overlapping, in each well. Sprinkle with any remaining cinnamon sugar.

Bake for 12–15 minutes, or until golden. Cool on a wire rack for 5 minutes. Meanwhile, melt the apricot conserve with the water in a microwave-safe dish in the microwave for 20 seconds, then spread onto the still-warm biscuits before serving.

White Chocolate Chip & Apple Cookies

This simple recipe is so good to eat! The white chocolate helps to bring out the flavour of the apple and also helps with the setting of the biscuits. The grated apple needs to be squeezed out really well to get the best results. If the apple turns slightly brown don't worry – it adds a nice colour to the cookies.

Makes 

Gluten-free

For the gluten-free flour mix (makes 200g):
140g fine white rice flour
40g potato flour
20g tapioca flour

100g cooking margarine
¼ teaspoon baking powder
100g caster sugar
2 large pinches ground ginger
1 medium egg, at room temperature
1 medium Bramley apple, grated and thoroughly squeezed out
60g white chocolate, finely chopped

Preheat the oven to 200°C/400°F/gas mark 6. Line two baking trays with baking parchment (you will need to cook these in batches).

Mix all the flours together very thoroughly or put into a food processor and pulse until mixed.

Then place the flour mixture, margarine, baking powder, sugar and ginger into a food processor and blitz well. Add the egg and bring together, then transfer to a medium mixing bowl.

Add the squeezed-out apple and chopped chocolate, and mix really well. Roll the dough into a 15–20cm long sausage shape, then wrap in clingfilm and chill for 15 minutes.

Scoop off 5–8mm thick sections of the chilled dough roll with a palette knife or spoon (you won't get neat slices because the dough will still be quite soft). Place the cookies on the lined trays and bake in the oven for 15–20 minutes, or until lightly browned.

Once cooked, allow the cookies to cool slightly on the trays, then transfer to a wire rack to cool completely. Store the cooled biscuits in an airtight container for up to 1 week.

The dough and the cooked cookies freeze well. For the dough: Wrap it in clingfilm and freeze. Defrost for 1 hour or until soft enough to cut and cook as above. For the cookies: Wrap well and store in an airtight container. Defrost for 30 minutes, then heat through at 180°C/350°F/gas mark 4 for 2–3 minutes to soften again.

Gluten-free Almond Jam Cookies

These delicious gluten-free cookies have a nutty almond flavor combined with sweet strawberry jam. An old family recipe, these are great with a glass of peach iced tea.

Makes 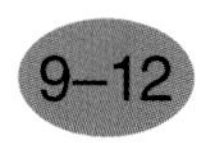

Gluten-free 

Vegan

115g butter substitute
45g evaporated cane juice
1 teaspoon vanilla extract
¼ teaspoon almond extract

For the gluten-free flour mix (makes 145g):
100g white rice flour
35g potato starch
15g tapioca starch
1½ teaspoons xanthan gum

¼ teaspoon salt
1½ teaspoons egg replacer, whisked with 2 tablespoons warm water
45g finely chopped almonds
170g organic strawberry jam

Preheat the oven to 180°C/350°F/gas mark 4. Line two baking trays with foil or baking parchment.

Using a stand mixer, cream the butter substitute and cane juice until light and fluffy. Add the vanilla and almond extracts, mixing until combined. Stop the machine and scrape down the sides and bottom of the bowl. Then add the flour and salt. Mix on a medium speed for 30 seconds. Stop and scrape down the sides of bowl again. Add the egg replacer and mix for 30 seconds until a ball of dough forms. Wrap the cookie dough in clingfilm and refrigerate for 1 hour.

Once the dough is chilled, roll it into 2.5cm balls, flouring your hands as necessary. Spread the chopped almonds on a baking tray, then roll the balls through them to cover on all sides. Press your thumb into the centre of each ball, fill with half a teaspoon of jam, and place on the prepared baking trays.

Bake the cookies for 12–14 minutes or until they have browned. Place on wire racks to cool. Store in an airtight container.

Pecan Shortbread Cookies

Known by many names, such as Mexican Wedding Cookies, Russian Tea Cookies or Snowman Cookies, these treats are loved by all. This vegan version tastes just as good as the regular recipe.

Makes 24 V Vegan

225g butter substitute
170g evaporated cane juice
260g unbleached plain flour
¼ teaspoon salt
175g shelled pecan nuts, finely chopped
2 teaspoons vanilla extract
70g organic icing sugar

Preheat the oven to 180°C/350°F/gas mark 4. Line two baking trays with foil or baking parchment.

Using a hand-held electric whisk, beat together the butter substitute and cane juice on a high speed for about 2 minutes until light and fluffy. Stop and scrape down the sides of the bowl. Add the flour, salt, pecans, and vanilla extract and mix for 30 seconds until a ball of dough forms. If the dough is too soft to roll, cover with clingfilm and refrigerate for 1 hour.

Roll the dough into 2.5cm balls, flouring your hands as necessary, and place on the prepared baking trays.

Bake the cookies for 10–12 minutes. Cool on wire racks. Once cooled, roll in the icing sugar. Store in an airtight container at room temperature, or freeze, in an airtight container or freezer bag, for up to three months.

Orange Tuiles

These light crisp biscuits look impressive, are easy to make and are great with ice cream and mousses. They will soften if they are kept in a moist atmosphere so, as soon as they are cold, store in an airtight tin. They are shaped like curved tiles, hence the name ('tuile' is French for tile).

- 2 organic egg whites
- 110g caster sugar
- 50g butter
- 50g plain flour, sifted
- zest of 1 unwaxed orange, grated

Preheat the oven to 190°C/375°F/gas mark 5.Line a baking tray with baking parchment.

Whisk the egg whites until quite stiff and add the caster sugar. Continue to whisk until smooth and glossy.

Melt the butter and add it to the egg white mixture by degrees, together with the sifted flour. Fold in the orange zest.

Spread out teaspoonfuls, well apart, on the baking tray and bake for about 5–6 minutes, until pale brown.

Drape the tuiles over a rolling pin to make them round. Cool on a wire rack.

Sweet Potato Thins

It's not often you use sweet potato in cakes or biscuits, but the sweet flavour and texture make a great cookie and it also works well in cakes. A little baking powder will lighten the texture of the biscuit, but the end result should be thin and crisp.

Makes   Gluten-free

1 large sweet potato, approximately 100g

For the gluten-free flour mix (makes 150g):
105g fine white rice flour
30g potato flour
15g tapioca flour

1 teaspoon baking powder
pinch of salt
40g caster sugar
50g cooking margarine
1 medium egg, at room temperature
sieved icing sugar and ground allspice, for dusting

Preheat the oven to 160°C/325°F/gas mark 3.

Bake the sweet potato for 50 minutes until soft. Cool slightly, then peel and mash with a fork. Set the mash aside to cool completely.

Place the flour mix, baking powder, salt, sugar and margarine into a medium mixing bowl and gently rub together, or place in a food processor and pulse until you have achieved the consistency of fine breadcrumbs. Add the egg and cold sweet potato and mix well.

Then roll the dough into a 15–20cm long sausage and chill in the fridge for at least 1 hour.

When the dough is chilled, and you are ready to cook the biscuits, line a baking tray with baking parchment (you will need to cook these in batches).

Cut the dough into 5mm slices and place on the tray. Flatten out with your fingers until about 3mm thick, or thinner if possible.

Bake for 18–20 minutes, or until lightly browned and crisp, then leave to cool on the tray or on a wire rack.

Serve dusted with icing sugar and ground allspice.

Store the cooled biscuits in an airtight container for up to 1 week.

The raw dough freezes well. Wrap it in clingfilm and freeze. Defrost for 1 hour or until soft enough to cut and cook as above.

Savoury Flavours

Parmesan Shortbread

These make the perfect accompaniment to pre-dinner drinks since they are sufficiently salty to get those gastric juices going, but simple enough not to detract from the main event – the dinner. Make sure you use freshly grated Parmesan for the best flavour.

Makes 

85g fresh Parmesan cheese, finely grated
85g plain flour, sifted
¼ teaspoon salt
70g unsalted butter, creamed until very soft
2 teaspoons olive oil

Preheat the oven to 150°C/300°F/gas mark 2. Lightly grease a baking tray.

Mix all the ingredients together in a bowl until well combined then gather the mixture together with your hands.

Roll out to along sausage-shape, about 23cm long. Try to make it as round a shape as possible. Set on a plate in the refrigerator for at least 30 minutes.

After this time, cut into thin slices using a very sharp knife and set on the baking tray. Bake in the oven for 20–25 minutes or until pale golden brown.

Transfer to a wire rack and allow to cool before eating.

Pepper Biscuits

If you know Astrid Lindgren's world famous children's books, you will recognise these Swedish cookies known as pepperkakor. The dough is very easy to make, and can also be shaped into ***pebernødder*** ('pepper nuts') – small, round, crispy biscuits the size of a cobnut.

Makes many cookies!

250g soft salted butter
500g sugar
200ml whipping cream
200ml golden syrup
2 tablespoons baking powder
4 teaspoons ground ginger
4 teaspoons ground cinnamon
4 tablespoons cocoa powder
4 teaspoons ground cardamom
2 teaspoons ground black pepper
approx. 1 kg plain flour
royal icing sugar, to decorate

Blend the butter and sugar in a mixer, or in a big bowl. Stir in the cream, followed by the rest of the ingredients except the flour. Add the flour until the dough is no longer sticky. Knead it well, then let the dough rest in the fridge overnight.

The next day preheat the oven to 180°C/350°F/gas mark 4.

Roll the dough to a very thin sheet (2mm thick is fine), and cut into shapes. Remember to pierce holes in the biscuits if you want to use them for hanging decorations. Arrange on baking parchment until the last scrap is used. Bake in the oven until golden.

Decorate with royal icing. The traditional way is to frame the biscuit, make buttons, shoes and so on, and to write the family's names on heart-shaped biscuits and hang them in the windows on red ribbons.

Oatmeal Crackers

One should never be without oatmeal crackers. This recipe is a little unusual as the dough is made with oatmeal and olive oil and they turn out wonderfully crisp. Roll thinly and choose a 'house style' for your crackers.

Makes  20

125g fine oatmeal
100g medium oatmeal
¼ teaspoon bicarbonate of soda
¼ teaspoon salt
1 tablespoon olive oil
150ml warm water

Preheat the oven to 160°C/325°F/gas mark 3. Grease and flour a couple of baking trays.

Measure the dry ingredients into a bowl – the fine and medium oatmeal, the bicarbonate of soda and the salt. Stir to mix.

Add the olive oil to the warm water, give it a stir then pour it into the dry mix. Stir with the handle of a wooden spoon until the mixture forms a soft dough.

Sprinkle a little fine oatmeal on a clean work surface and roll out the dough to about 5mm thick. You can cut the rolled dough into squares with a knife or use a round biscuit cutter to shape.

Place the shaped crackers on a baking tray, prick with a fork and bake for 15–20 minutes. For a crisp result, turn them over halfway through baking. When cooled, remove from the baking trays and cool on a wire rack, then store in a biscuit tin until required.

Uncooked, shaped crackers can be frozen for up to 3 months. When required, place frozen dough shapes on a prepared baking tray and bake from frozen.

Cheese Sablés

Buttery, crumbly, cheesy, just a little spicy these elegant bites are absolutely perfect with a glass of chilled white wine. Coat the outside of these biscuits with a mixture of sesame and kalonji seeds to create a sophisticated cocktail nibble.

Makes about 

- 175g plain flour, plus extra for dusting
- 1 teaspoon sea salt
- ½ teaspoon cayenne pepper
- ½ teaspoon dry mustard powder
- 1 teaspoon cumin or caraway seeds, lightly crushed
- freshly ground black pepper
- 150g unsalted butter, chilled and diced
- 75g finely grated mature Cheddar cheese
- 75g finely grated Parmesan cheese
- 1 tablespoon milk
- sesame seeds (optional)
- kalonji (black onion) seeds (optional)

Tip the flour, salt, cayenne, mustard powder, cumin or caraway seeds and some black pepper into the bowl of a food processor. Add the diced butter and use the pulse button to rub it into the dry ingredients. Add the grated cheeses and pulse again until the dough just comes together – you may need to add a drop of cold water.

Tip the dough out onto a lightly floured work surface and roll into a log roughly 5cm in diameter, wrap in clingfilm and chill in the fridge for a couple of hours or until firm.

Preheat the oven to 180°C/350°F/gas mark 4 and line a baking sheet with non-stick baking parchment.

Take the log out of the fridge, remove the clingfilm and brush with milk before coating in the sesame and kalonji seeds (if using). Slice the log into discs, roughly 5mm thick, and arrange on the baking sheets, spacing the biscuits well apart.

Bake on the middle shelf of the preheated oven for 12–15 minutes, or until crisp and golden. Once completely cold, the sablés can be packaged.

Stored in an airtight box, they will keep for 4–5 days.

After Dinner Treats

Brown Caramel Biscuits

With their slight bitter tinge, these biscuits are for grown-ups. The recipe also involves precision, the dough starting off as caramel, to which the rest of the ingredients are added. The biscuits have a very special porous crispness due to the potassium carbonate, or potash, used. As this recipe makes a lot of biscuits, the dough keeps well, wrapped in the fridge, and also freezes well.

Makes 24

500g sugar
250g golden syrup
500g salted butter
15g potash (available from chemists)
50ml beer
125g blanched almonds, roughly chopped
15g ground cinnamon
7g ground cloves
5g ground ginger
1 blade of mace, ground
150g candied peel from a cedrate (a large lemon relative) or other candied peel, cut into 1cm dice
grated zest of 1½ lemons
1kg plain flour

Preheat the oven to 180°C/350°F/gas mark 4. Line a baking tray with baking parchment.

Melt the sugar, syrup and butter in a thick-bottomed pot. When it boils, remove from the heat and leave to cool. Dissolve the potash completely in a little beer: it emits a foul odour, but this disappears in a short while.

When the sugar mixture has cooled slightly, mix in the potash, almonds and spices. Cool some more, until just below room temperature. Mix in the candied peel, grated zest and flour. If you do not follow these instructions carefully, the dough will separate, or it will become a solid caramel, and you will have to start over by melting it again.

Roll the dough into fat sausages, wrap in several layers of wax paper and clingfilm and cool completely in the fridge.

Cut into slices as thin as you can manage with a very sharp knife. Bake until the biscuits are just baked through. The crispness comes when they are cooled. If they do not crisp up, bake them some more; but they must not burn or they will be indelibly bitter. Store in airtight tins.

Chocolate-drenched Cocoa-nib Cookies

Cocoa nibs are widely available online or from specialist chocolate shops; alternatively, use chocolate chips, or even nibbed almonds for a nutty version.

Makes 12

225g unsalted butter
150g demerara sugar
pinch of sea salt
250g plain flour
100g dark cocoa powder
½ vanilla pod, the seeds scraped out, or ½ teaspoon vanilla extract
1 medium free-range egg
50–100g cocoa nibs (as many as you like), or chocolate chips
300g Venezuelan dark chocolate, or your favourite robust dark chocolate

Preheat the oven to 180°C/350°F/gas mark 4. Line a baking tray with baking parchment.

Place the butter, sugar and salt in a saucepan and melt thoroughly. Remove from the heat and add the flour, cocoa powder, vanilla seeds (or extract) and the egg, mixing thoroughly. Add the cocoa nibs and allow the cookie dough to cool for 5 minutes.

Place generous scoops of the dough on the lined baking tray, leaving 7.5cm between each cookie. You'll probably need to bake in two or three batches. Bake for 8–10 minutes, then leave to cool completely.

Once you have baked your cookies and resisted eating them all while warm, the next step is to drench them in chocolate. Chop the dark chocolate into 1cm pieces and place in a bainmarie to melt slowly until smooth and lump-free.

Dip half of each cookie in the tempered chocolate and place back on the parchment paper to let the chocolate cool and set fully.

Store the cookies in an airtight container or leave on a plate for everyone to eat while fresh. They won't last long.

Macaroons

These lovely old-fashioned macaroons are easy to make and keep for ages.

Makes 

110g ground almonds
175g caster sugar
2 small organic egg whites
¼ teaspoon pure almond extract
a little granulated sugar
24–26 blanched almonds

Preheat the oven to 180°C/350°F/gas mark 4. Line two baking trays with baking parchment.

Put the almonds and sugar in a bowl. Whisk the egg whites lightly and mix into the dry ingredients, a little at a time. Add the almond extract and beat well to make a fairly smooth, stiff mixture.

Spoon the mixture onto the trays in lumps the size of a walnut.

Sprinkle with sugar and decorate each with an almond. Place in the oven and bake for 10–15 minutes, or until just firm.

Cool for a few minutes, then lift off the tray and cool on a wire rack.

Chocolate & Hazelnut Drops

This cookie crumbles in your mouth and carries just enough chocolate and hazelnuts to make it into the perfect-bite category.

Makes 24

250g butter, softened
120g caster sugar
300g plain flour
1 teaspoon baking powder
80g good-quality dark chocolate chips (minimum 70% cocoa solids)
70g hazelnuts, roughly chopped

Preheat the oven to 180°C/350°F/gas mark 4.

Put the butter and sugar in a large bowl and cream together with a wooden spoon until pale in colour. Sift in the flour and baking powder, and then add the chocolate chips and hazelnuts. Bring the mixture together to form a dough.

Using your hands, roll the dough into small drops and place them slightly apart on two baking trays (there is no need to grease or line).

Flatten the chips slightly with the back of a damp fork and bake in the oven for 13–15 minutes or until they are light golden brown and slightly firm on the top.

Carefully transfer the drops to a wire rack to cool.

Double Dark Chocolate, Pecan & Ginger Cookies

These are very grown-up cookies, with a double hit of chocolate and just a hint of ginger. If you prefer swap the ginger for candied orange peel or dried cherries.

Makes 20

325g dark chocolate
125g unsalted butter
200g light muscovado or soft light brown sugar
3 large eggs
1 teaspoon vanilla extract
150g plain flour
½ teaspoon baking powder
1 tablespoon cocoa
pinch of salt
100g pecans, chopped
1 rounded tablespoon finely chopped stem ginger

Break 200g of the chocolate into pieces and melt it with the butter, either in a heatproof bowl set over a pan of barely simmering water or in the microwave on a low setting. Stir until smooth and set aside to cool slightly. Chop the remaining chocolate into chunks.

Whisk the sugar and eggs together in a large bowl for a couple of minutes. Add the vanilla extract, then the melted chocolate and butter mixture, and stir until smooth. Sift together the flour, baking powder, cocoa and salt. Add to the cookie mixture with the chopped chocolate, pecans and stem ginger and mix until thoroughly combined. Cover with clingfilm and chill for a couple of hours, until firm.

Preheat the oven to 180°C/350°F/gas mark 4 and line two baking trays with non-stick baking parchment. Using a dessertspoon, scoop balls of the cookie mixture onto the baking trays, leaving space between them.

Flatten the cookies slightly and bake in batches on the middle shelf of the oven for about 12 minutes, until firm but not crisp. Remove from the oven and let the cookies cool on the trays.

Repeat with the remaining cookie dough. Cool the cookies completely before packaging.

Stored in an airtight container, they will keep for about five days.

Chocolate Brazil Soft Baked Biscuits

A Brazil nut has the calorie content of half an egg and is especially rich in amino acids so you may feel a mixture of guilt and contentment as you tuck into these delicious biscuits.

Makes 20

75g unsalted butter
60g caster sugar
1 large egg, beaten
175g wholemeal self-raising flour
½ teaspoon vanilla extract
1–2 tablespoons milk
75g dark chocolate (minimum 60% cocoa solids), roughly chopped
50g Brazil nuts, chopped
pinch of salt

Preheat the oven to 180°C/350°F/gas mark 4. Grease a baking tray with melted butter.

Cream together the butter and sugar in a bowl until light and fluffy. Beat in the egg. Sift the flour once, returning the bran from the wholemeal flour that has remained in the sieve to the sifted flour, then fold it into the mixture. The bran gives a distinctive flavour and texture. Beat well, adding the vanilla extract and sufficient milk to make a pliable dough. Mix it with your hands, adding the milk in stages until the dough is fairly soft, but not sticky.

Add the chopped chocolate, nuts and salt and distribute evenly through the dough. Roll out onto a lightly floured board to a thickness of about 5mm. Stamp into rounds and place the biscuits, spaced well apart, on the greased baking tray.

Bake in the centre of the oven for about 20 minutes. Watch them carefully so they don't overcook.

Remove from the oven and leave to cool on the baking tray for a few minutes before transferring to a wire rack to cool completely.

Chocolate Water Biscuits for Cheese

These unusual yet well-balanced crackers are the perfect pairing for many varieties of cheese, whether English, French, blue, goat's or hard. You can give texture and extra flavour to the biscuits by adding dried herbs or spices, such as fennel or cumin seeds, black pepper and chilli.

250g plain flour
1 teaspoon sea salt
20g cocoa powder
½ teaspoon English mustard powder (optional)
any choice of spice or herb (optional)
85g butter

Put a jug of water to chill in the fridge for 30 minutes.

Place all the dry ingredients (including any flavourings) in a large bowl and mix well. Rub in the butter until evenly combined. Gradually add enough refrigerated water to form a pliable dough; this must not be too sticky, so be careful when adding the water. Knead the dough gently until smooth. Wrap in clingfilm and refrigerate for 30 minutes to rest and relax.

Preheat the oven to 180°C/350°F/gas 4. Roll the dough on a well-floured surface to 3mm thick or thereabouts. Use a round cutter to cut out circles of your preferred size, e.g. a 2.5 cm cutter for canapé-size biscuits, or 5cm for cheese biscuits; alternatively, use a sharp knife to cut into squares or rectangles. Prick each biscuit with a fork and bake until golden and crisp, about 10–12 minutes. Place on a wire rack to cool.

The biscuits can be stored in an airtight container for two to three months.

Festive Delights

Fortune Cookies

Fill each of these cookies with a personalised message of goodwill and give them to your family and friends at New Year or any other significant event. Bake the cookies in small quantities, as you have to work very quickly to fill and shape them once they come out of the oven before the delicate mixture becomes too dry and brittle and then impossible to fold.

Makes about  12

100g plain flour
pinch of ground ginger
pinch of salt
3 large egg whites
100g icing sugar
1 teaspoon vanilla extract
75g unsalted butter, melted and cooled slightly

Preheat the oven to 150°C/300°F/gas mark 2 and line two baking trays with non-stick baking parchment.

Sift together the flour, ground ginger and salt. In a medium-sized bowl, whisk the egg whites until foamy. Add the icing sugar and vanilla extract and whisk until combined. Stir in the sifted dry ingredients, then add the melted butter and mix until smooth. Set aside for 10 minutes.

Draw two 10cm diameter circles on each sheet of baking parchment and spoon 1 tablespoon of the mixture on to each circle. Using either the back of a spoon or a palette knife, spread the mixture in an even layer to fill the circles.

Bake one tray on the middle shelf of the preheated oven and the other on the shelf below for about 6–8 minutes, until the cookies are starting to turn golden at the edges.

Working quickly, remove one tray of baking parchment from the oven at a time, leaving the other baking tray inside and, using a palette knife, carefully and quickly lift the cookies off the parchment. Flip the cookie over, lay your fortune message in the middle and fold the cookie over it in half. Bring the points of the cookie together to make the fortune cookie curl and leave to cool in a muffin tin (this will help them to keep their shape). Repeat with the remaining cookies.

Once you have used up all of the mixture and all of your cookies are baked and shaped, slide the muffin tin into the oven for a further minute to brown them evenly.

Leave to cool in the tins before packaging in takeaway boxes. Stored in an airtight container, they will keep for up to three days.

Ginger Snapdragon Cookies

For an extra special occasion decorate the top of each of these super gingery cookies with a small square of fine edible gold leaf, which is available in small books from sugarcraft or baking suppliers.

200g unsalted butter, softened
125g caster sugar
175g golden syrup
75g black treacle
1 large egg, beaten
425g self-raising flour
1 teaspoon bicarbonate of soda
4–5 teaspoons ground ginger
large pinch of cayenne pepper
pinch of salt
2 nuggets of stem ginger, finely chopped

Preheat the oven to 180°C/350°F/gas mark 4 and line two baking trays with non-stick baking parchment.

Cream together the softened butter and caster sugar until light and fluffy. Add the golden syrup, treacle and beaten egg and mix until smooth. Sift together the dry ingredients and stir into the mixture. Add the chopped stem ginger and mix again until thoroughly combined.

Using two spoons, place walnut-sized balls of the mixture on the prepared baking trays, spacing them well apart to allow enough space for them to spread during cooking.

Bake in batches on the middle shelf for about 10–12 minutes, or until the cookies are golden brown – the edges should be crisp and the middle still slightly soft. Cool completely before packaging.

Stored in an airtight box or biscuit tin, these will keep for four or five days.

Jane's Biscuits

A great little recipe because it is quick and its formula of 2/4/5 is easy to remember. The flavour is quite different if you use unsalted butter, but still delicious.

50g caster sugar
110g butter
175g white flour

Preheat the oven to 180ºC/350ºF/gas mark 4. Line a baking tray with baking parchment.

Put the flour and sugar into a bowl and rub in the butter until you have a fine breadcrumb mix.

Gather the mixture together and knead it lightly. Roll out to 5mm thick. Cut into rounds with a 6cm cutter or into heart shapes. Arrange on the baking tray and bake for 10–15 minutes until pale brown.

Remove and cool on a wire rack. Serve with fruit fools, compotes and ice creams.

Deluxe Florentines

These delicate fruit and nut biscuits are perfect served with tea or coffee.

Makes  16

50g flaked almonds
25g hazelnuts, roughly chopped
25g mixed peel, chopped
50g glacé cherries, roughly chopped
50g seedless raisins
75g butter
75g soft light brown sugar
75g plain chocolate, melted
75g white chocolate, melted

Preheat the oven to 180°C/350°F/gas mark 4. Line a baking tray with baking parchment.

Mix together the nuts, peel, cherries and raisins.

Melt the butter in a saucepan, stir in the sugar and heat gently, stirring until the sugar has dissolved. Continue to heat until the mixture just starts to bubble.

Remove the pan from the heat and add the fruit and nuts. Stir well.

Place spoonfuls of the mixture onto the prepared baking tray, leaving sufficient space between each for spreading.

Bake in batches in the preheated oven for 10–12 minutes until golden brown.

As soon as the tray is removed from the oven, use a knife to tidy any uneven edges, making a neat round shape. Allow to cool a little. When firm, place on a wire rack until cold.

Use the melted chocolate to coat the flat side of the florentines, using plain chocolate on half the florentines and white chocolate on the others. Using a fork, draw wavy lines on the chocolate. Leave until set.

Gingerbread Biscuits

Decorate the cooked biscuits with white icing or gild with edible gold leaf, then wrap as gifts or thread with ribbon to decorate the Christmas tree.

Makes  18

225 plain flour
½ teaspoon mixed spice
1 teaspoon ground ginger
1 teaspoon ground cinnamon
½ teaspoon salt
½ teaspoon bicarbonate of soda
100g butter
75g soft brown sugar
3 tablespoons golden syrup

For the icing:
1 egg white
1 teaspoon lemon juice
500g icing sugar, sifted

Preheat the oven to 160°C/325°F/gas mark 3. Lightly grease a baking tray or line with baking parchment.

Sift the flour, spices, salt and bicarbonate of soda into a large bowl. Use a metal spoon to mix lightly. Place the butter, sugar and syrup in a medium saucepan and melt over a low heat, stirring occasionally.

Make a well in the centre of the dry ingredients and pour in the melted butter and sugar mixture and mix together. When the mixture has formed a ball, turn it out onto a clean dry surface and roll out to a thickness of 3mm.

Dip biscuit cutters lightly into flour and cut out shapes. Place on the baking tray. If you wish to thread the finished biscuits with ribbon, use a drinking straw to cut a hole in each shape.

Bake for 10–12 minutes until golden brown, then remove from the oven and place the biscuits on a wire rack to cool.

To make the icing, whip the egg white lightly, add the lemon juice and stir. Add the icing sugar a spoonful at a time until you have a good consistency. Use a piping bag and a writing nozzle to decorate the biscuits.

Cinnamon Spice & All Things Nice Cookies

Serve these spciy biscuits with a coffee or as a dessert with roasted apple wedges and a dollop of Greek yogurt.

Makes 30

250g butter, softened
80g caster sugar
½ can condensed milk
1 teaspoon vanilla extract
360g plain flour
2 teaspoons baking powder
3 teaspoons ground cinnamon
125g dried apple rings, finely chopped

Preheat the oven to 180°C/350°F/gas mark 4. Line a baking tray with baking parchment or use a non-stick tray.

Cream the butter and sugar together until pale and smooth, add the condensed milk and vanilla extract and mix until combined. Sift in the flour, baking powder and cinnamon and then add the dried apple and mix to form a dough. Roll into a cylinder, approximately 4cm in diameter (at this stage you can refrigerate the dough and use as and when required).

Slice the dough into round pieces 1cm thick and place on a baking tray, leaving a gap between each. Cook for 15–20 minutes until golden.

Speculaas

On St Nicholas' Day (5 December), the Dutch tradition is to bake and eat special little spice biscuits called speculaas. These are flavoured with spices – cinnamon, nutmeg and cloves – added in an exact ratio. Sometimes, nibbed almonds and grated orange or lemon zest are added.

255g plain flour
a pinch of bicarbonate of soda
a pinch of salt
170g unsalted butter, cut into cubes
140g soft light brown sugar
½ teaspoon ground cinnamon
¼ teaspoon grated nutmeg
¼ teaspoon ground cloves
a little grated orange or lemon zest (optional)
55g nibbed almonds (optional)
about 3 tablespoons milk

Sift the flour and bicarbonate of soda into a bowl. Add the salt. Rub in the butter until the mixture resembles breadcrumbs. Stir in the sugar, then add the spices and, if you are using them, the citrus zest and almonds.

Stir in just enough milk to combine to a stiff dough. Shape into a ball with your hands and wrap in clingfilm. Chill in the refrigerator overnight (or for at least 2 hours).

Preheat the oven to 180°C/350°F/gas mark 4. Lightly grease a baking tray.

Roll out the dough to a thickness of 1cm, then cut into shapes using a pastry cutter. If you use an 8cm pastry cutter, you can make 24–28 biscuits.

Place on the baking tray and bake in the oven for about 20 minutes, or until they are still slightly soft to the touch.

Transfer to a wire rack to cool completely, during which time the biscuits will become crisp and firm. Store in an airtight container.

Star of Bethlehem Biscuits

A guiding light for Santa as well as the Magi, leave these out with the essential nip of something fiery or a glass of milk and a pile of moss and carrots for the reindeers on Christmas Eve.

Makes approx. 

140g plain flour
60g golden caster sugar
120g unsalted butter, diced
¼ teaspoon vanilla extract
1 medium egg yolk, beaten
10g cocoa, sifted
groundnut or vegetable oil for brushing
20g dark chocolate (approx. 70% cocoa solids), broken into pieces
icing sugar for dusting (optional)

Place 80g of the flour, half the sugar and half the butter in the bowl of a food processor and briefly whizz until the mixture is crumb-like. Add the vanilla and half the egg yolk and whizz again until the mixture comes together into a ball. Wrap in clingfilm and chill for at least an hour.

Make a second batch of dough with the remaining flour, sugar, butter and egg yolk in the same way, adding the cocoa to the food processor with the flour (and omitting any vanilla). Chill this too.

Preheat the oven to 170°C fan/190°C/gas mark 5, and brush a couple of baking trays with oil. Thinly roll out each dough in turn on a lightly floured work surface, rotating it as necessary, very lightly sprinkling the top with a little flour to stop the rolling pin sticking. Cut out stars using a 6cm cutter and arrange on baking trays, rolling the dough twice. Bake for about 10 minutes, until lightly coloured, then remove and immediately loosen with a metal spatula – if you leave them even a few minutes they will break as you remove them. Leave to cool.

Gently melt the chocolate in a small saucepan over a low heat. Using a pastry brush, dab a little in the centre of each vanilla biscuit, then sandwich with a chocolate one so the points of the stars are alternated. If you like, lightly dust the tops with icing sugar, using a tea-strainer.

Set aside in a cool place for about an hour for the chocolate to harden. These will keep well in an airtight container for several days.

Stained Glass Snowflake Cookies

These look beautiful hanging at a window, allowing the light to shine through the 'stained glass'. Or you could give one cookie to each guest as a place setting or table gift for the Christmas dinner table.

Makes 

225g unsalted butter, softened
150g icing sugar
1 large egg, beaten
1 teaspoon vanilla extract
350g plain flour, plus extra for rolling
pinch of salt
assorted flavoured and coloured boiled sweets

Preheat the oven to 180°C/350°F/gas mark 4 and line two baking trays with non-stick baking parchment.

Cream the softened butter and icing sugar together until pale and light. Add the whole egg and vanilla extract and mix again until thoroughly combined. Sift the flour with the salt, add to the bowl and mix again until smooth.

Gather the dough into a ball, flatten into a disc and wrap in clingfilm. Chill for a couple of hours, or until firm.

Meanwhile divide the boiled sweets into separate colours, place in freezer bags and crush using a rolling pin.

Lightly dust a work surface with flour and roll out the dough until it is roughly 3mm thick. Using snowflake cutters, stamp out snowflakes in assorted sizes and arrange on the prepared baking trays. Carefully and neatly fill the holes in the snowflakes with the crushed boiled sweets. Bake in batches on the middle shelf of the preheated oven for about 12 minutes, until the cookies are pale golden and the boiled sweets have melted and filled the holes.

Cool the cookies on the trays until hardened, and package into boxes lined with greaseproof or waxed paper once completely cold. These will keep for four or five days in an airtight box.

Christmas Tree Biscuits

It's worth saving the hanging of these biscuits until Christmas Eve or just before, not only to keep them fresh, as they soften within a day, but because, as with tree chocolates, the tree will have been denuded come Christmas Day. You will need a set of cutters – anything from holly leaves, bells, snowflakes, snowmen, stockings and stars – and some thin ribbon for hanging them.

50g unsalted butter
100g golden caster sugar
100g runny honey
225g plain flour
½ teaspoon baking powder
½ teaspoon bicarbonate of soda
1 teaspoon each ground ginger and cinnamon
½ beaten medium egg
vegetable oil for brushing
white writing icing, to decorate
silver balls (optional)

Gently heat the butter, sugar and honey together in a small saucepan, stirring until melted and smooth. Working off the heat, add the dry ingredients and stir until crumbly, then add the egg and work to a dough. If it seems very sticky you can add a little more flour. Tip this on to a work surface, bring it into a ball, then pat it between your palms until you have a pleasingly smooth and shiny dough. Wrap it in clingfilm, leave to cool, then chill for several hours or overnight.

Preheat the oven to 180°C/350°F/gas mark 4, and brush a couple of baking trays with vegetable oil.

Thinly roll out the dough on a lightly floured work surface to a thickness of about 2mm and cut out the desired shapes using biscuit cutters. Roll the dough twice, arranging the biscuits on the baking trays – they don't spread much, so you can place them quite close together. If you are planning on hanging them, make a hole at the top of each one using a skewer.

Bake the biscuits for 10–12 minutes until an even pale gold; the lower tray may take longer than the upper one. The holes will have closed up a little, so make them a bit larger using the skewer. Now loosen the biscuits with a palette knife – it's important to do this straight away, before they harden and become brittle. Transfer to a rack to cool.

Ice and decorate them as you fancy, and leave to set for an hour or two. They can be stored in an airtight container, un-iced or iced, for several weeks. Thread them with thin ribbon if you are planning on hanging them.

Christmas Cookie Dough

Cookie dough makes a delicious and thoughtful gift all year. Patterned wrapping paper, stationery and cheerful scraps of paper look so lovely wrapped around logs of cookie dough that have been bundled in waxed or greaseproof paper.

Makes  rolls

250g butter, softened
120g caster sugar
300g plain flour
1 teaspoon baking powder
80g white chocolate, chopped
70g dried cranberries, chopped

Put the butter and sugar in a large bowl and cream together with a wooden spoon until pale in colour. Sift the flour and baking powder, then add the white chocolate and dried cranberries. Bring the mixture together to form a dough.

Cut the dough into three. Roll each third into a sausage shape. Wrap in greaseproof paper, cover with another wrap of Christmas gift-wrapping paper and tie at both ends with some pretty ribbon.

The cookie dough can be cut into 8 pieces and then baked for 10–15 minutes in a preheated oven at 180°C/350°F/gas mark 4. The dough should be stored in the fridge and will keep for up to a week.

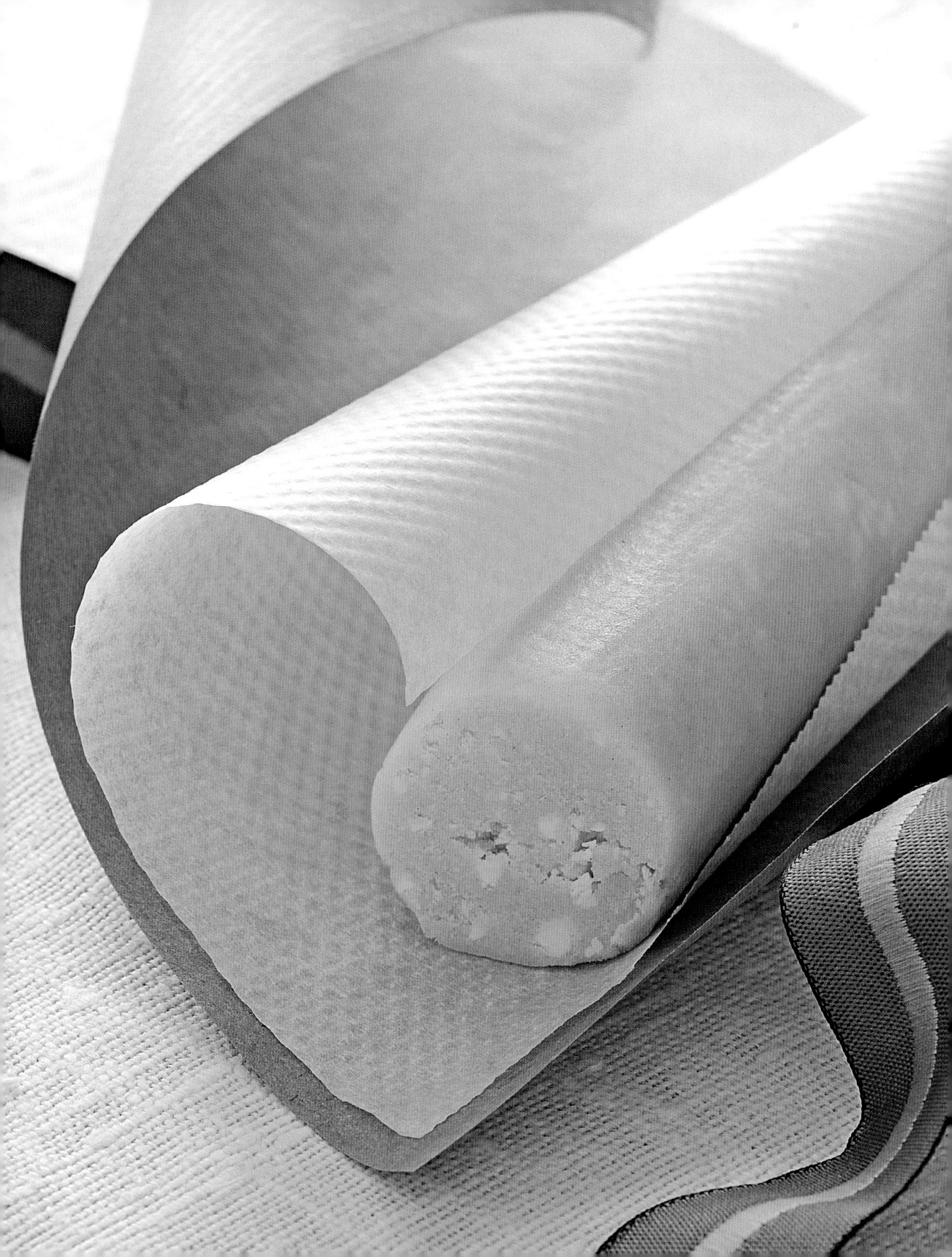

INDEX

Recipe Acknowledgements

We would like to thank the following authors for kind permission to reproduce their recipes:

Chapter 1: Afternoon Tea

p.12 Jammy Dodgers from *On Baking* by Sue Lawrence
p.15 Vanilla Cookie Sandwiches from *On Baking* by Sue Lawrence
p.16 Orange Butter Biscuits from *Forgotten Skills of Cooking* by Darina Allen
p.19 Nut and Butter Biscuits from *Forgotten Skills of Cooking* by Darina Allen
p.20 Chocolate Meringue 'S' biscuits from *Bake!* by Nick Malgieri
p.23 Breton Butter Biscuits from *Green & Black's Chocolate Recipes* written and compiled by Caroline Jeremy
p.24 Chocolate Shortbread from *On Baking* by Sue Lawrence
p.27 Vanilla Almond Fluted Biscuits from *Scandinavian Kitchen* by Camilla Plum
p.28 Pecan Puffs from *Darina Allen's Ballymaloe Cookery Course* by Darina Allen
p.31 Lana's Coffee & Walnut Biscuits from *Forgotten Skills of Cooking* by Darina Allen
p.32 Aztec Cookies from *On Baking* by Sue Lawrence
p.35 Anzac Biscuits from *On Baking* by Sue Lawrence
p.37 Chocolate Peanut Butter & Fudge Cakes from *Seriously Good! Gluten-Free Baking* by Phil Vickery
p.38 Chocolate Digestive Biscuits from *Sweet Vegan* by Emily Mainquist
p.41 Mother-in-Law's Tongues from *Darina Allen's Ballymaloe Cookery Course* by Darina Allen
p.42 Lemon Cookies from *Perfect Parties* by Alison Price
p.45 Date, Walnut & Lemon Cookies (© Splenda/McNeil Nutritional Ltd) from *The Sweet Life* by Anthony Worrall Thompson
p.46 Lemon & Pistachio Biscotti from *Party Party Party!* edited by Kyle Cathie
p.49 Orange and Almond Biscotti from *Homemade* by Clodagh McKenna
p.50 Lavender Biscuits from *Jekka's Complete Herb Book* by Jekka McVicar

Chapter 2: Healthier Choices

p.54 Soft Zesty Lemon Fondant Cookies from *Seriously Good! Gluten-Free Baking* by Phil Vickery
p.57 Soft Pine Nut Cookies from *Seriously Good! Gluten-Free Baking* by Phil Vickery
p.58 Peach Biscuits from *Sweet Vegan* by Emily Mainquist
p.61 White Chocolate Chip & Apple Cookies from *Seriously Good! Gluten-Free Baking* by Phil Vickery
p.62 Gluten-free Almond Jam Cookies from *Sweet Vegan* by Emily Mainquist

p.65 Pecan Shortbread Cookies from *Sweet Vegan* by Emily Mainquist
p.66 Orange Tuiles from Darina *Allen's Ballymaloe Cookery Course* by Darina Allen
p.69 Sweet Potato Thins from *Seriously Good! Gluten-Free Baking* by Phil Vickery

Chapter 3: Savoury Flavours
p.73 Parmesan Shortbread from *On Baking* by Sue Lawrence
p.74 Pepper Biscuits from *Scandinavian Kitchen* by Camilla Plum
p.77 Oatmeal Crackers from *From Mother to Daughter* by Vivienne Bolton
p.78 Cheese Sablés from *Gifts from the Kitchen* by Annie Rigg

Chapter 4: After Dinner Treats
p.83 Brown Caramel Biscuits from *Scandinavian Kitchen* by Camilla Plum
p.84 Chocolate-drenched Cocoa-nib Cookies from *Adventures with Chocolate* by Paul A. Young
p.87 Macaroons from *Darina Allen's Ballymaloe Cookery Course* from Darina Allen
p.88 Chocolate & Hazelnut Drops from *Homemade* by Clodagh McKenna
p.91 Double Dark Chocolate, Pecan & Ginger Cookies from *Gifts from the Kitchen* by Annie Rigg
p.92 Chocolate Brazil Soft Baked Biscuits from *Green & Black's Chocolate Recipes* written and compiled by Caroline Jeremy
p.95 Chocolate Water Biscuits for Cheese from *Adventures with Chocolate* by Paul A. Young

Chapter 5: Festive Delights
p.99 Fortune Cookies from *Gifts from the Kitchen* by Annie Rigg
p.100 Ginger Snapdragon Cookies from *Gifts from the Kitchen* by Annie Rigg
p.102 Jane's Biscuits from *Ballymaloe Cookery Course* by Darina Allen
p.105 Deluxe Florentines from *Party Party Party!* edited by Kyle Cathie
p.106 Gingerbread Biscuits from *From Mother to Daughter* by Vivienne Bolton
p.109 Cinnamon Spice & All Things Nice Cookies from *The Modern Vegetarian* by Maria Elia
p.110 Speculaas from *On Baking* by Sue Lawrence
p.113 Star of Bethlehem Biscuits from *Gorgeous Christmas* by Annie Bell
p.114 Stained Glass Snowflake Cookies from *Gifts from the Kitchen* by Annie Rigg
p.117 Christmas Tree Biscuits from *Gorgeous Christmas* by Annie Bell
p.118 Christmas Cookie Dough from *Homemade* by Clodagh McKenna

Photography Acknowledgements

We would like to thank the following photographers for kind permission to reproduce their images:

p.2, pp.4-5, p.6, p.7, p.9 William Shaw

Chapter 1: Afternoon Tea
p.13, p.14, p.17, p.18 William Shaw
p.21 Quentin Bacon from *Bake!* by Nick Malgieri
p.22 Francesca Yorke from *Green & Blacks Chocolate Recipes* written and compiled by Caroline Jeremy
p.25 William Shaw
p.27 Anne-Li Engström from *The Scandinavian Kitchen* by Camilla Plum
p.29, p.30 William Shaw
p.33, p.35 Jean Cazals from *On Baking* by Sue Lawrence
p.36 Tara Fisher from *Seriously Good! Gluten-free Baking* by Phil Vickery
p.39 Penny de Los Santos from *Sweet Vegan* by Emily Mainquist
p.41, p.43 William Shaw
p.44 Steve Baxter (© Splenda/McNeil Nutritional Ltd) from *The Sweet Life* by Anthony Worrall Thompson
p.47 Gus Filgate from *Party Party Party!* edited by Kyle Cathie
p.48, p.51 William Shaw

Chapter 2: Healthier Choices
p.55, p.56 Tara Fisher from *Seriously Good! Gluten-free Baking* by Phil Vickery
p.59 Penny de Los Santos from *Sweet Vegan* by Emily Mainquist
p.60 Tara Fisher from *Seriously Good! Gluten-free Baking* by Phil Vickery
p.62 Penny de Los Santos from *Sweet Vegan* by Emily Mainquist
p.64, p.67 William Shaw
p.68 Tara Fisher from *Seriously Good! Gluten-free Baking* by Phil Vickery

Chapter 3: Savoury Flavours
p.72 William Shaw
p.75 Anne-Li Engström from *The Scandinavian Kitchen* by Camilla Plum
p.76 Catherine Gratwicke from *From Mother to Daughter* by Vivienne Bolton
p.79 Catherine Gratwicke from *Gifts from the Kitchen* by Annie Rigg

Chapter 4: After Dinner Treats

p.82 William Shaw
p.85 Anders Schonnemann from *Adventures with Chocolate* by Paul A. Young
p.86 William Shaw
p.89 Alberto Peroli from *Homemade* by Clodagh McKenna
p.90 Catherine Gratwicke from *Gifts from the Kitchen* by Annie Rigg
p.93 Francesca Yorke from *Green & Blacks Chocolate Recipes* written and compiled by Caroline Jeremy
p.94 Anders Schonnemann from *Adventures with Chocolate* by Paul A. Young

Chapter 5: Festive Delights

p.98, p.101 Catherine Gratwicke from *Gifts from the Kitchen* by Annie Rigg
p.103 Ray Main from *Ballymaloe Cookery Course* by Darina Allen
p.104 William Shaw
p.107 Catherine Gratwicke from *From Mother to Daughter* by Vivienne Bolton
p.108, p.111 William Shaw
p.112 Chris Alack from *Gorgeous Christmas* by Annie Bell
p.115 Catherine Gratwicke from *Gifts from the Kitchen* by Annie Rigg
p.116 Chris Alack from *Gorgeous Christmas* by Annie Bell
p.119 Alberto Peroli from *Homemade* by Clodagh McKenna

p.128 William Shaw